Introducing
Famous
Americans

T0022517

Meet

Sitting Bull

Lakota Chief

Enslow Publishing
101 W. 23rd Street
Suite 240
New York, NY 10011
USA
enslow.com

Jane Katirgis and Chris Hayhurst

Published in 2020 by Enslow Publishing, LLC
101 W. 23rd Street, Suite 240, New York, NY 10011

Cataloging-in-Publication Data

Names: Katirgis, Jane. | Hayhurst, Chris.
Title: Meet Sitting Bull: Lakota chief / Jane Katirgis and Chris Hayhurst.
Description: New York : Enslow Publishing, 2020. | Series: Introducing famous Americans | Includes bibliographical references and index. | Audience: Grades 3–5.
Identifiers: ISBN 9781978511361 (library bound) | ISBN 9781978511347 (pbk.) | ISBN 9781978511354 (6 pack)
Subjects: LCSH: Sitting Bull, 1831–1890—Juvenile literature. | Dakota Indians—Biography—Juvenile literature. | Hunkpapa Indians—Biography—Juvenile literature. | Little Bighorn, Battle of the, Mont., 1876—Juvenile literature.
Classification: LCC E99.D1 K37 2020 | DDC 978.004/9752440092 [B]—dc23

Printed in the United States of America

To Our Readers: We have done our best to make sure all website addresses in this book were active and appropriate when we went to press. However, the author and the publisher have no control over and assume no liability for the material available on those websites or on any websites they may link to. Any comments or suggestions can be sent by email to customerservice@enslow.com.

Portions of this book originally appeared in *Sitting Bull: Sioux War Chief*.

Photo Credits: Cover, p. 1 (Sitting Bull) Niday Picture Library/Alamy Stock Photo; cover, p. 1 (background illustration) De Agostini Picture Library/Getty Images; pp. 4, 15, 16, 20, 23, 25, 26 Library of Congress Prints and Photographs Division; pp. 5, 19, 22, 24 The Denver Public Library, Western History Collection, call numbers B-74, X-33793, B-750, B-793; p. 7 (top) Hulton Archive/Archive Photos/Getty Images; p. 7 (bottom) Library of Congress Geography and Map Division; p. 8 Geoffrey Clements/Corbis Historical/Getty Images; p. 9 Smithsonian American Art Museum, Washington, DC/Art Resource, NY; p. 10 Hulton Archive/Getty Images; p. 11 Historical Picture Archive/Corbis Historical/Getty Images; pp. 12, 17 © North Wind Picture Archives; p. 13 Marilyn Angel Wynn/Nativestock/ Getty Images; p. 14 Werner Forman/Universal Images Group/Getty Images; p. 21 (top) Private Collection/The Stapleton Collection/Bridgeman Images; p. 21 (bottom) GraphicaArtis/ Archive Photos/Getty Images; interior pages background pattern and graphic elements Ambient Ideas/Shutterstock.com.

Contents

1 Early Life 4

2 Bravery 11

3 Sitting Bull and the
Lakota Sioux 16

4 Ghost Dance and
Standing Rock 22

Timeline 27

Glossary 28

Learn More 29

Primary Source Image List 30

Index 32

① Early Life

Sitting Bull began his life with the name Jumping Badger. He was born in 1831 along the Grand River in present-day South Dakota. While his mother, a Native American woman, gave birth, his father, a Lakota Sioux warrior, stood nearby.

Sitting Bull sits with one of his wives in front of a tepee. The Sioux were nomadic people and camped wherever the buffalo were.

A studio photograph taken in the 1880s shows Sitting Bull after the Battle of Little Bighorn and his surrender to the US Army.

Jumping Badger seemed different from other children in the Hunkpapa Lakota tribe. He moved slowly and thought deeply before acting. Soon he was given the nickname Hunkesni, which means "slow." But Hunkesni was certainly not slow. As he grew up, he was quick to master important skills.

Let's Learn More

The name given to Sitting Bull, Tatanka Iyotanka, was chosen to reflect his firmness and courage. It describes a buffalo sitting on its haunches and refusing to move.

Native Americans sit on their horses. American Indian men were taught to ride well at an early age. *Right*: A map of the Dakota Territory. The Black Hills are in the western part of the territory.

One of the skills Hunkesni mastered was hunting. The Hunkpapa tribe and all the Lakota people hunted buffalo for food. The great animal was also a source of clothing, shelter, and bedding. Hunting buffalo was a way of life for the Lakota. Hunkesni killed his first buffalo when he was ten years old.

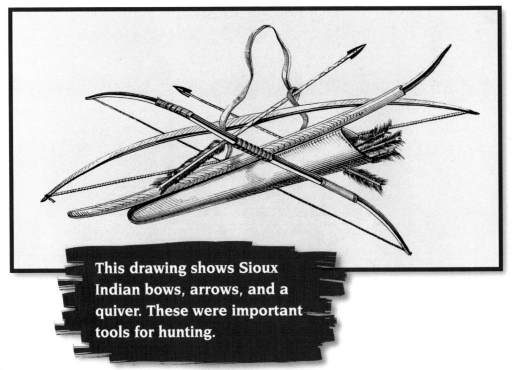

This drawing shows Sioux Indian bows, arrows, and a quiver. These were important tools for hunting.

Artist John M. Stanley (1814–1872) created this painting of a buffalo hunt on the prairie.

The buffalo was so important to the Lakota that it often led them to war. Other Native American tribes also hunted buffalo. Sometimes their hunting grounds overlapped. The tribes fought each other for the buffalo and the land where they lived. It was important for Lakota boys to learn to fight.

Notice the buffalo hides that are being cleaned and dried at the right of this sketch depicting a Native American village by the artist George Catlin (1796–1872).

② Bravery

Hunkesni was a brave young man. At age fourteen, he and a group of Lakota warriors went to a river. They found a band of Crow warriors by the water. Hunkesni, leading the way, was the first Lakota to strike. He knocked a Crow off his horse. Within minutes, almost all the Crow warriors were dead.

Native American artist Amos Bad Heart Buffalo painted this picture of dancing sometime around 1890.

At a special ceremony, Hunkesni's father congratulated his son for his bravery. Then, to honor his becoming a man, he gave him his name. Hunkesni would now be known as Tatanka Iyotanka—Sitting Bull.

This Native American warrior examines the fallen enemy after a skirmish between different tribes.

Sioux warriors' shirts were dyed with local pigments and adorned with quill work and hair.

In 1857, Sitting Bull was named war chief of the Hunkpapa tribe. He was also recognized as a holy man, or Wichasha Wakan.

The Hunkpapa believed Sitting Bull had great spiritual powers. A great leader was exactly what they needed. A new threat—far greater than the Crow—was upon them.

Sioux chiefs wore an eagle feather warbonnet. Sitting Bull is pictured wearing such a bonnet on page 5.

White settlers used any excuse to kill buffalo because Native Americans depended on them for food. Here, hunters shoot buffalo that appear to block the passage of a train.

Let's Learn More

Native Americans obtained almost everything they needed from the buffalo. It fed them. It provided skins for clothing and tepees. Its sinews were used to make string for arrows.

Sitting Bull and the Lakota Sioux

3

White people were nothing new to Sitting Bull. He had seen them all his life. Sometimes the whites and the Lakota would meet to trade. Other times they would fight. The real goal of the whites was gold and new territory. They felt they had a right to Native American land.

The settlement of the West enriched many white Americans. In this magazine cartoon, a white American carries bags full of the huge profits he made at the expense of the starving Native American to his left.

Shown here are Native Americans trading buffalo hides for gunpowder, sugar, tea, and other goods at the trading post.

In 1868, the Lakota elected Sitting Bull leader of the entire tribe. Sitting Bull worked hard to unite his people. In the winter of 1876, soldiers attacked and destroyed a Native American camp. They forced the surviving Native Americans out into the cold. Sitting Bull saw this as an act of war.

Let's Learn More

Sitting Bull and the Lakota Sioux were told to move to reservations because gold had been discovered on their land. The expedition that made the discovery was led by George Armstrong Custer.

In an address to his followers, Sitting Bull calls for resistance against US demands that his people move out of the Black Hills.

On June 25, 1876, Major General George Armstrong Custer led his troops in an attack on the Lakota people. But Custer and his men were outnumbered. The Lakota, led by Sitting Bull, killed Custer and nearly all his men. But the US Army kept attacking the Lakota and wore them down. One by one the Lakota tribes surrendered. Sitting Bull had to give in.

The reckless behavior of Major General George Armstrong Custer, shown here, won battles during the Civil War but led him to disaster at the Little Bighorn.

Above: The retreat of Major Reno's command by the Native American artist Amos Bad Heart Buffalo. *Below*: The grandly heroic painting of Custer's last stand by Edgar Paxson.

4 Ghost Dance and Standing Rock

Standing Rock Reservation was run by the US government. Sitting Bull and his Lakota tribe were sent to live there.

One day, members of the government came to Sitting Bull's reservation to explain that parts of the reservation would now be open to whites. Sitting Bull was angry.

This photograph shows one of Sitting Bull's trials at the Indian Agency on the Standing Rock Reservation. Sitting Bull was accused of urging various tribes to resist white demands.

Sitting Bull and William "Buffalo Bill" Cody are shown in a studio portrait from 1885. Sitting Bull briefly worked with Cody in his Wild West show before returning to Sioux territory.

The Lakota began performing a sacred ceremony called the Ghost Dance. They thought the dance would rid their land of white people forever and bring back the traditional way of life. American soldiers quickly forbade the Ghost Dance, but the Native Americans danced anyway.

Sitting Bull's two wives and daughters were photographed sometime in the 1880s.

Ghost Dance and Standing Rock

In this image, Sioux Indians perform the Ghost Dance.

Back at Standing Rock Reservation, the government feared that Sitting Bull would bring the Ghost Dance to his people. On December 15, 1890, they sent Native American policemen to Sitting Bull's home to arrest him. They dragged him outside. In the confusion, a fight erupted. Shots rang out. Sitting Bull was dead.

The grave site of Sitting Bull is near Mobridge, South Dakota. By the time Sitting Bull died, the Indian Wars were over and most tribes were confined to reservations.

Timeline

1831 — Sitting Bull is born near the Grand River.

1845 — Sitting Bull fights his first battle and is honored by his tribe as a warrior.

1857 — Sitting Bull is named war chief of the Hunkpapa Lakota Sioux.

1868 — Sitting Bull is elected head chief of the Lakota Sioux.

1876 — War begins between the Lakota Sioux and the United States Army.

1880s — Sitting Bull and his tribe are forced to live on a reservation.

1890 — Sitting Bull is murdered as he is arrested by reservation police.

Glossary

ceremony (SER-ih-moh-nee) A special celebration done on certain occasions.

chief (CHEEF) A leader of a Native American tribe or nation.

expedition (ek-spuh-DIH-shun) A trip for a special purpose.

forbid (fur-BID) To not allow.

Hunkpapa (HUHNK-pah-puh) A tribe of the Lakota Indians.

reservation (reh-zer-VAY-shun) An area of land set aside by the government for a special purpose.

sinew (SIN-yoo) A strong band of living tissue that joins muscle to bone.

surrender (suh-REN-der) To give up.

warrior (WAR-ee-yur) One who goes into battle.

Learn More

Books

LaPlante, Walter. *Sitting Bull*. New York, NY: Gareth Stevens Publishing, 2016.

Stillman, Deanne. *Blood Brothers: The Story of the Strange Friendship Between Sitting Bull and Buffalo Bill*. New York, NY: Simon & Schuster, 2017.

Strand, Jennifer. *Sitting Bull*. Minneapolis, MN: ABDO Zoom, 2018.

Websites

History for Kids
historyforkids.net/sitting-bull.html
Read about the brave man recognized for his courage.

Kiddle
kids.kiddle.co/Standing_Rock_Indian_Reservation
Read facts about Standing Rock Reservation.

Kids Connect
kidskonnect.com/people/sitting-bull
Check out more Sitting Bull facts and worksheets.

Primary Source Image List

Page 4: Photograph copyright Bailey, Dix & Mead, 1882.

Page 5: Photograph by David Francis Barry, 1880s.

Page 7: Top: A stereograph of Native Americans on horseback, c. 1880. Bottom: *Rice's Sectional Map of Dakota Territory*, by Fred Sturnegk, 1872.

Page 8: Sioux Indian bows and arrows, drawn by Karl Bodmer in the 1830s.

Page 9: *Buffalo Hunt on the Southwestern Prairies*, by John M. Stanley, oil on canvas, 1845.

Page 10: Drawing of an Indian village based on *Sioux Camp Scene*, by George Catlin, 1841.

Page 11: *Dance in Honor of the Warrior He Dog*, by Amos Bad Heart Buffalo, c. 1890.

Page 12: Hand-colored woodcut of an illustration by Frederic Remington.

Page 15: *Shooting Buffalo*, from *Frank Leslie's Illustrated Newspaper*. June 3, 1871.

Page 16: *The reason of the Indian outbreak General Miles declares that the Indians are starved into rebellion*. Cartoon from *Judge*, 1890.

Page 19: *Sitting Bull Addresses His Followers*, from *Kelsey's History of the Wild West*, published between 1880 and 1890.

Primary Source Image List

Page 20: George Armstrong Custer, photographed by Matthew Brady before 1865.

Page 21: Top: *The Retreat of Major Reno's Command*, by Amos Bad Heart Buffalo (1869–1913). Bottom: *Custer's Last Stand*, by Edgar S. Paxson, 1899.

Page 22: The Standing Rock Indian Reservation, photographed by David Francis Barry in 1886.

Page 23: Sitting Bull and William Cody, photographed in 1885 by David Francis Barry.

Page 24: Photograph of Sitting Bull's wives and daughters, taken by David Francis Barry in the 1880s.

Page 25: *Ghost Dance of the Sioux Indians in North America*. Illustration in *The Illustrated London News*, 1891.

Index

B

bravery, 11, 12
buffalo, 8, 10, 15

C

ceremonies, 12, 24
Crow tribe, 11, 14
Custer, George Armstrong, 18, 20

G

Ghost Dance, 24, 26
gold, 16, 18
Grand River, 4

H

Hunkesni, 6, 8, 11, 12
Hunkpapa Lakota tribe, 6, 14
hunting, 8

J

Jumping Badger, 4, 6

L

Lakota tribe, 4, 6, 10, 11, 16, 18, 20, 22, 24
land/territory, 10, 16, 18, 24

S

Sitting Bull, 12, 14, 16, 18, 20, 22
South Dakota, 4
Standing Rock Reservation, 22, 26

U

US Army/soldiers, 20, 24
US government, 22, 26

W

whites, 16, 18, 22